Morning Magic

Arrmon Abedikichi

No part of this book may be reproduced in any form without written permission from the author. Reviewers may quote brief excerpts from the book in reviews.

Disclaimer: No part of this publication may be reproduced or transmitted in any form, mechanical or electronic, including photocopied or recorded, or by any information storage and retrieval system, or transmitted by email without permission in writing or email from the author or publisher.

While attempts have been made to verify all information provided in this publication, neither the author nor the publisher assumes any responsibility for errors, omissions, or contrary interpretations of the subjects discussed.

This book is for entertainment purposes only. The views expressed are those of the author alone and should not be taken as expert instructions or commands. The reader is responsible for his/her own actions.

Adherence to all applicable laws and regulations, including international, federal, state, and local government, or any other jurisdiction is the sole responsibility of the purchaser or reader.

Neither the author nor the publisher assume any responsibility or liability whatsoever on the behalf of the purchaser or reader of these materials.

Any perceived slight of any individual or organization is purely unintentional.

Copyright © 2016 Arrmon Abedikichi

All rights reserved.

ISBN-13: 978-1534682979
ISBN-10: 153468297X

Free Gift

Morning Magic Starter Kit

As a way of showing my gratitude for your purchase, I am offering you a FREE book that is exclusive only to book readers. **It is the companion guide for this book.**

In the *Morning Magic Starter Kit*, you'll find a guide to dreaming, planning, and creating your own perfect morning routine. It includes charts for tracking habits, creating affirmations, a sleep journal and much more. It is sure to "level-up" your mornings.

Download your copy for free:

www.levelupstar.com/morningmagic

TABLE OF CONTENTS

Free Gift iv

My Failures... 1

I am 100% Responsible 6

What is a Morning Routine? 10

    What is Your Morning Routine? 12

Understanding Your Habits 14

5 Reason You Aren't a Morning Person 21

The 4 Pillars of Morning Magic 28

Pillar #1: Night Time Rituals 30

    14 Night Time Ritual Ideas 32

Pillar #2: High-Quality Sleep 40

    Simple & Effective Sleep Hacks 48

    Top 10 Things to Avoid Before Bed 54

Pillar #3: Waking Up Productive 57

    11 Productive Wake Up Strategies 59

Pillar #4: Morning Magic 65

Samples of Morning Routines 69

    Start the Day with Success 71

Creating Your Morning Magic 74

    Chart Your Morning.. 74

    50+ Morning Activity Ideas 77

    Top 10 Things to Avoid in the Morning 81

Stick-to-it-ness 84

    8 Powerful Tips to Make it Stick................................. 85

Review, Tweak, Modify 92

    Weekly Review 94

    Tweak and Modify 95

Putting Everything Together 97

Moving Forward 98

Would You Like to Know More? 101

About the Author 103

Bibliography 105

Notes 107

www.levelupstar.com

My Failures...

For the majority of my life I was setting myself up for failure each and every day. The worst part of it was that I had no idea that I was sabotaging myself so badly. In my own reality, I was doing what I thought everyone did.

Here is what I was doing...

I would wake up in the morning to an annoying alarm. It was the sound of that generic preset alarm tone on your cell phone that you grow to hate over time. That dreaded noise became a tone I had a strong dislike for even if it came from someone else's phone.

The first action of the day would be to snooze at least 2-3 times on a normal day. Some days it could be even more. You know how it is. That extra few minutes of low quality sleep can really energize you for the rest of the day, right?

After multiple snoozes, I would lay in bed dreading the day ahead. My mind would be racing with thoughts like, *"What am I going to wear? I wish I could sleep for just 30 more minutes. Today is going to be a crappy day. I do not want to go to work/school."*

The next agenda would be to check social media. Ahhh yes. Let me see what everyone else is doing. Let me check up on the latest gossip. There I would mindlessly like, reply, and comment to anything in my news feed. Those cute kitten videos can really eat up your time.

Just like clockwork, next would be email. Against my own will, I had to open the inbox just in case there was some super important email I had to check up on and reply to immediately. Nevertheless, I would spend precious minutes replying to other people's "to-do lists" creating more stress and anxiety for myself. Furthermore, it made me quite aware of more things I "needed" to do.

I was able to complete all of this before I even got out of bed. This left me in a panicked rush for the rest of the morning (adding even more stress). I still had to get up, shower, eat, pick out what to wear, get dressed, and adjust for traffic conditions.

Can you relate to this?

If so, I know exactly how you feel. If you have ever said the statement, "*I am not a morning person*" then this book is for you. To be honest, this was never even meant to be a book at all. It all started as a personal experiment on myself. I never considered myself to be a morning person until I started studying success. I had to do something drastic to change my own behavior and outcomes.

There is one constant amongst the majority of successful people I have been studying. They all have some type of morning routine and they are mostly early risers. Is there some type of special magic in morning air? I wanted to find out. That led me on an exhaustive study and countless experiments.

Who am I?

My name is Arrmon Abedikichi. I run the blog www.levelupstar.com. The purpose of my website is to share ideas, tips, and strategies that will help you "level-up" your life and become a better version of yourself. I study and share simple and effective strategies that anyone can easily implement in their life. Regardless of who you are or where you come from, you can always improve. Growth is the essence of life.

In January 2014, I lost everything in a merciless house fire. I was very lucky to even get out alive. All I was left with was the shirt on my back. That was my wake up call. It made me very aware of the mediocre life I was living. I had been stuck in a zombie-like routine for years. I knew I had more to give in this life, but I was scared. What if I failed? What would others think about me? At that point, I really did not have much else to lose. I realized I had two options: Give up or fight.

I chose to fight. I knew I could no longer live the way I was living. I needed to become a better version of myself. That would require me to "level-up" my life in all areas. That led me to study success from all angles and dissect the commonalities. I made it a point to learn from anyone that was "successful". I would study their approach and ask better questions.

This book has been in the making my entire life. I have made many necessary mistakes that led me to look for solutions. I have been knocked back, beat up, and slowed down. I have experienced countless failures, and I have learned from them.

This book is the basis of it all. How you start your day determines the mood of your day. How you live your days determines the direction of your life. The direction of your life determines where your life goes.

In this book you will learn:

- Benefits of a morning routine
- What stops you from being a "morning person"
- How to become a morning person
- How to sleep better and wake up feeling refreshed

- The 4 pillars of *Morning Magic*
- How to create your own *Moring Magic*
- And much more!

By creating a meaningful morning routine, I have completely changed my life and YOU can too! It is possible to wake up excited for the day like a kid on Christmas morning. It is possible to get more done before 8 AM than most people do all day. It is possible to tweak a few things in your bedroom and get the best sleep of your life. All of this is completely within your grasp.

We will cover all of these topics in this book and many more. Before we get started, I want to share with you a concept that completely changed my outlook on life. This is very important on your journey to level-up your mornings, your sleep, and your life. It all starts with YOU.

I am 100% Responsible

"The man who complains about the way the ball bounces is likely to be the one who dropped it."

– Lou Holtz

If your life is not where you want it to be, then why not? I am sure there are plenty of valid reasons such as: the economy is bad, no one is hiring, someone cheated you, the timing was off, you did not know the right people, you were not born with the skill/talent, you do not have the money or time, etc.

First of all, let me say I know from experience how this feels. It can make you feel helpless. These were just a few of my excuses for years. These "excuses" were woven into my story and no one could tell me otherwise.

A few years ago, I came across an old book that a teacher suggested I read when I was in high school. When she recommended the book, I did not think anything of it and never intended to read it. It was Stephen Covey's, *The 7 Habits of Highly Effective People: Powerful Lessons in Personal Change*. A few years ago, this book magically found its way back into my life again, so I decided to read it.

Covey discusses seven habits that can have a profound effect on one's life. As I began to read, the first habit had a very strong impact on me. It was the complete opposite of how I had been living my life. I was immediately drawn in because it made so much sense to me as I read through the text. I knew I had been violating the first habit.

Be Proactive.

Being proactive is the ability to control your own environment, rather than having it control you. We all have the power to decide how to respond to conditions and circumstances rather than react.

A great example is: It is raining therefore today is a bad day. Do exterior events that are out of your control really dictate your day so profoundly? That is for you to decide.

Another example: Jessica said some really mean things about me. *She makes me so mad.* Did she actually "make you feel mad" or did you choose to feel mad based on what she said and what that means to you? You can decide how to react to external stimuli. No one makes you choose how to feel.

You do not have the ability to control other people's actions, but you do have 100% control over the things you *think, say, and do.*

Proactivity is taking responsibility for your life. You cannot always control what others do but you can control how you respond to what happens. How we act accordingly affects how things impact us.

People who lack proactivity tend to be very reactive. They see themselves as victims. When this happens, they feel powerless and give up the ability to change their circumstances. It seems much easier to blame others for their problems than to take responsibility for them.

I considered myself a victim for many years. I felt powerless to change my life. I did not know what to do, where to start, or how to go about it. It was so overwhelming I decided to do nothing at all. That in itself was a choice. Luckily, I did not give up completely.

If you find yourself blaming others or denying responsibility for your results, then you may be a "victim" that is reacting rather than choosing to consciously act. One of the first steps to leveling-up your life is to take full responsibility for your results and choose to do something about it.

As we start this process of creating a morning routine, it is inevitable that problems will occur. It is not the problems that matter; it is how you deal with them. Be proactive. Claim 100% responsibility for your results. Even if you fall short, this gives you the power to change anything you do not like.

Just remember, failure is not forever. Failures can actually be a wonderful learning tool. It all depends on your perspective. I have learned much more from failure than I have from any success. Failure gives you experience. Experience brings with it knowledge. Knowledge is power, but only when it is acted upon.

Be solution-oriented. Focus on what is in your control. Take 100% responsibility for your wins and your losses. Be accountable for your results or lack thereof. Learn from your mistakes. Create opportunities, do not wait for them. Take control. *Be proactive.*

What is a Morning Routine?

"Lose an hour in the morning, and you will spend all day looking for it."

-Richard Whately

We all have a morning routine. Some are good and some are not so good. As I mentioned earlier, my old morning routine was absolutely horrendous. I had no clue it was having such a negative effect on my life until I became aware of it.

Are you aware of your morning routine? Most people mindlessly go through the same hurried and panicked steps every single day and think mornings are awful. When in reality, they have not taken the time to plan their mornings to be more efficient and effective.

How you start your day can dramatically affect your level of success in every area of your life. On the most basic level, you can set yourself up for success each and every day. You can become more productive, increase your happiness, improve your health, overcome procrastination, and become a better version of yourself. You can do all of this before most people even wake up. **Mornings can be magical**.

Most morning routines consist of waking up, getting dressed, preparing for work or school, and eating breakfast. Not all mornings are the same. Some people work nights and have different schedules. For all intents and purposes, we are talking about the period of time after you wake up to start your day.

The main purpose of setting an effective morning routine should be to give yourself "me time" and take charge of your day. During this time period, you can start the day with power and enthusiasm on your own terms.

Benefits of a Morning Routine

Here's the deal. When you wake up in the morning, you are refreshed and rejuvenated from a night's sleep. Think of yourself like your cell phone. You have been "plugged up" all night, and when you wake up, you are at 100% battery. As the day wears along, you drain your battery.

This also applies to your willpower. In the morning, you have the most focus and willpower. This is why it is important to use this time of day to do things that require a certain amount of willpower to accomplish rather than wait until the end of the day when you are tired and drained, mentally and physically.

I know what you must be thinking. This sounds great and all, but I just do not have enough time. I can relate. I have two children, and mornings can be hectic. Some days I feel like the ring leader of the circus, but this is why I choose to start my day before everyone is even awake. This special time for myself allows me to choose what to focus on before everyone requires my attention. To put it plain and simple, I focus on things that are important to me and things that will make me a better person.

What is Your Morning Routine?

In order to take control of your morning and start the day on your terms, you need to evaluate your current habits and behaviors. What is your morning routine?

It is time to document it. Do not be biased or judgmental. Simply observe yourself in the morning and take note of what you do and the order in which you do it. How long does each activity take?

Observe what is going on in your life each morning for a few days. For years I was going through the same routine daily without any awareness of how it affected my life. Are you doing the same? If so, document it. Become aware of what you are doing and the effect it is having on your life.

Awareness is a powerful tool. It allows you to see the bigger picture. You can get an elevated view of your life by being more aware of the choices you make and the effects they have on your life.

Tracking Your Current Routine

I've created the free, downloadable Morning Magic Starter Kit (please visit www.levelupstar.com/morningmagic). In it, you will find the "Morning Routine Tracking Chart". Use this chart to track your current morning routine for the next few days. Do not change anything about your behavior yet. Just observe and document what you do. Allow yourself to go through the "normal" motions of your morning without being biased to your results.

You will use this information later to get a better understanding of your habits and help you create the perfect morning routine.

Understanding Your Habits

"Successful people are simply those with successful habits."

– Brian Tracy

Our entire life is a sum of habits. We form our habits and then our habits form us. We, as humans, are habitual creatures. Habits make our lives much easier. They allow us to perform repeatable actions without having to process all the information every single time. Before we go any further, let's take a closer look at habits.

What exactly is a habit? A habit is a routine or behavior that is repeated regularly and tends to occur unconsciously. Did you catch the last part? Habits tend to occur unconsciously. For the most part, we follow through with our habits without even thinking about them. This is part of the reason they are so hard to break.

This is why tracking your habits is so powerful. It allows you to consciously examine them as they occur. You can gain a greater understanding of how they work, what triggers them, and how they play out. If you can measure it, you can manage it.

Habits are formed when a new behavior becomes automatic. The formation of a habit is based on information we acquire from our environment, how we act based on this information, and the pain or pleasure we receive from it. To make this simple, let's refer to this as the "habit loop".

A habit is comprised of three elements (the 3 R's):

1. Reminder
2. Reaction
3. Reward

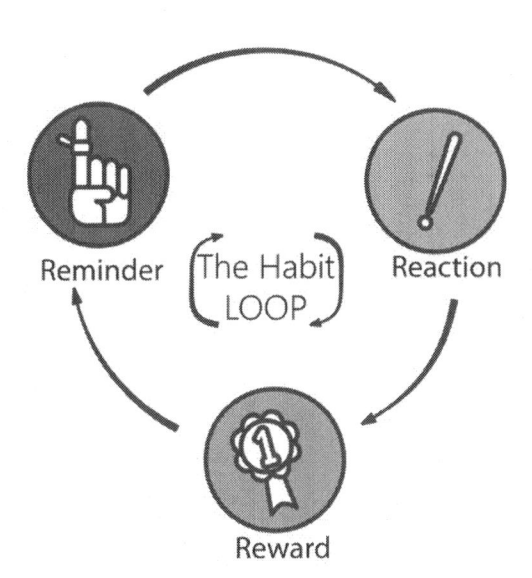

In the image above, you can see how the habit loop is an ongoing cycle. The reminder is a trigger that prompts a reaction that produces a reward. The reward reinforces the behavior and makes the prompting of the reminder even stronger.

Researchers at MIT (Smith & Ann, 2016) did several tests on lab rats in a maze. They would sound a buzzer and then allow the rat to freely navigate through the maze in search of chocolate. If the rat successfully found its way to the end, it was rewarded with the chocolate. After doing the test many times, the rats learned how to get to the chocolate (reward) with less and less effort as they memorized the path. Thus, over a period of time the activity in their brains decreased as they learned and memorized the process.

The rats were essentially running on autopilot when they had learned and remembered the correct path. Their brains recorded the repeated actions necessary to get to the chocolate and created a meaning behind the buzzer (reminder). They knew if they followed the correct path in the maze (reaction), they would be rewarded with a tasty treat at the end. Eventually they were just reacting to the noise because it meant they would soon have chocolate (reward). In reality, the noise had no affiliation with chocolate, only in the experiment.

Can you think of similar behavior in your own life? One thing immediately comes to mind for me. The sound of my alarm clock would instantly prompt a negative feeling for me. The sound meant pain because I had to get out of my comfortable bed and do things I did not enjoy. These types of "triggers" exist everywhere in our lives and most of the time we are not even aware of it.

Perspective on Habits

One of the main reasons I have suggested that you track your habits for a few days is so you can get an elevated view of your life. If you are honest with yourself and see how you regularly spend your time, you can take control of your life.

We unconsciously perform hundreds of habits daily without even thinking about it. Have you ever thought about how this directly affects your life and the lives of those around you?

Time is a currency just like money. You can save it, spend it, and invest it. The only difference is that time is much more valuable, because you cannot produce more of it. You cannot buy more time. You only have a limited amount of it. So how are you using your time?

Every human on Earth has the same amount of time allotted to them daily.

- 24 hours = 1,440 minutes
- 1 week = 168 hours or 10,080 minutes

- 30 days = 720 hours or 43,200 minutes
- 1 year = 8,760 hours or 525,600 minutes

When you break a week, month, or year down to hours or minutes, you can see it from a different perspective. If you are allotted 1,440 minutes per day, how are you using each minute?

Let's say you sleep eight hours a day. That leaves you 16 hours. Let's say you work eight hours and have a one hour commute in total. This leaves you seven hours in the day to do whatever you want.

According to Nielsen (Nielsen, 2014), in the average American was spending almost 5 hours per day watching television (4.7 hours to be exact). This is not even including smartphone or tablet usage. So let's do the math.

- 4.7 hours per day x 7 days per week = 32.9 hours per week
- 4.7 hours per day x 30 days a month = 141 hours per month
- 4.7 hours per day x 365 days per year = 1,715.5 hours per year

To put this in perspective, do you have any clue how many days 1,715.5 hours equals?

71.47 ENTIRE DAYS! That is 20% of the entire year spent sitting and watching television. That equates to 1/5 of the year wasted with nothing to show for it. Is this alarming to you? It absolutely blew my mind to find this out, because it was something that I was doing on a regular basis.

Do you see how a simple habit can have catastrophic consequences in your life without you even having a clue? Its small things like this that adds up. Being aware of your habits gives you the power and control to take your life back.

Awareness is the Key

Just by being aware of your habits can create massive leverage to change them. After you find out how destructive small habits can be, you will not need as much motivation to change them. It is by being aware that you gain lots of insight.

This same idea can apply for the positive habits in your life also. What if you spent 20 minutes a day reading? How many books could you read with an extra 121 hours (20 minutes per day x 365 days in a year) a year? What if you spent 20 minutes a day exercising? You could get in the best shape of your life in a matter of weeks or months.

The person that says they do not have enough time is lying to themselves and everyone else, but they are not aware of it. In their reality, it does seem like there is not enough time. In actuality, time can be managed better by cutting out a few small bad habits here and there. It is your responsibility to find out how you are using your time and what you are doing with it. If you want to create change, it starts with YOU.

Do the Math

Do you have any bad habits that you are aware of? How many times a day do you engage in this behavior? How many minutes of your time does it take? Do the math and figure out how much time per week, month, and year this behavior takes of your time. *Awareness is the first step in changing bad habits.*

5 Reason You Aren't a Morning Person

"Morning is wonderful. The only drawback is that it comes at such an inconvenient time of day."

–Glen Cook

Do you consider yourself a morning person? If you are reading this book, then the answer is probably no. Instead of jumping straight into "how to become a morning person" let's identify what is currently stopping you. If you know where the problem lies then you can do something to solve it.

If you do not consider yourself to be a morning person, what is stopping you? Take out a notebook and spend a few minutes to identify the causes. Make a list of reasons.

Did you make a list? Writing the reasons down might make them seem a little different than they were in your head. Waking up in the morning with energy and enthusiasm is something anyone can freely do, but there are often limiting beliefs that prevent that. When you are on autopilot, you just repeat the common habits you have been doing. Read over the list of reasons you just created. Are these legit reasons or merely excuses?

Through my own experimentation, I realized the biggest limiting factor in creating a morning routine was ME. I was my own worst enemy. It all depends on what you place the highest value on. If a few extra minutes of sleep are more important than doing something else in the morning, then of course you will take the few extra minutes of sleep. This is why it is important to identify your reasons why you do not consider yourself to be a morning person.

Here are the five most common reasons why people do not consider themselves to be a morning person. Do any of them sound familiar?

1. Limiting Beliefs and Self-Talk

Have any of these statements run through your head or come out of your mouth?

- I am not a morning person.
- I hate mornings.
- I am always tired.
- I cannot do it. It is impossible.
- I am not the type of person that can deal with change easily.

We hear them all the time. If you are affirming these types of statements constantly then this will become your reality. Your self-talk dictates your limiting beliefs.

Henry Ford said it best with his statement, *"If you believe you can or you can't, either way you are right."*

What kind of dialogue are you having in your head? Is it uplifting you or detrimental to your improvement? The way you communicate with yourself can have a big effect on your results.

Review your list of reasons why you are not a morning person one more time. I think it is fair to say that most of your reasons are probably limiting beliefs. Do these beliefs empower you or are they holding you back? Your limiting beliefs are a part of the story you tell yourself. Your "story" becomes your life. **You can change the story**.

Create empowering statements to replace those negative beliefs and self-talk. The next time you catch yourself engaging in negative self-talk, replace your statement with something that gives you strength and power.

For instance, if you were to say, "I'm always late." Replace it with, "I always arrive at least 10 minutes early." Reaffirm things in a positive tone that empowers you. Start living the part. Make it a point to arrive early everywhere you go. It all starts with a decision to take action. Become the person right now. It will start to change your thoughts and belief patterns. You can use this technique for any area of your life where you have negative self-talk and beliefs.

2. Habits

After tracking your morning habits for a few days, you should have a better understanding of how you are operating. This will give you the awareness and power to change things that you do not like. You do not have to operate on autopilot anymore. You can consciously decide what you want to do and how you will go about doing it.

Habits are very intriguing to me. Doing something one time does not usually create lasting change, but if you repeat it constantly over a period of time it becomes too big to ignore. For instance, if you eat healthy and exercise only once, you will not see any results. If you do both for six months straight, you will see massive results.

The chains of habits are very weak until they are too strong to be broken. Remember the definition of a habit from earlier? A habit is a routine of behavior that is repeated regularly and tends to occur **unconsciously**. Once you have done something so many times, you begin to do it on autopilot without even thinking about it.

This is why it is very important to decide your habits instead of letting them just happen. You can consciously choose healthy and powerful habits that will improve your life for the better.

You do have the power to change your habits and choose what to replace them with.

3. No Schedule or Agenda

Another reason why most people do not consider themselves to be a morning person is because they do not have a plan for the morning. The only plan is to get as much sleep as possible and get ready in time to make it where ever they need to be. If you fail to plan then you plan to fail.

I can look back at my old routine and see this as a major issue. If you do not have a plan, then you will engage in whatever comes up. This is reaction mode. For me, it could have been an email or a funny cat video on Facebook while I was lying in bed. Instead of letting your morning happen to you, we will create a plan to make your morning happen for you.

4. Overwhelm

Mornings can be hectic, especially if you have kids. Believe me, I know how it is! This is evermore the reason why you want to create a morning routine for yourself.

Overwhelm and overload creates stress. When we are stressed we start reacting to things instead of consciously making decisions. When this happens we will revert back to our old ways.

Trying to take on too many things at once can also create overwhelm. We want to make things simple and take baby steps. Rome was not built in one day and you do not have to be perfect. We will create a plan that will work for you and your circumstances. Start small. Build momentum.

5. Lacking a Reason Why

Why do you want to create a morning routine? Is there a specific reason? For some, it could be to gain more control over their lives. For others, it could be to start working out or being more productive. Whatever your reason is, it does not matter as long as you know why you are doing it.

It is best to create a compelling reason that will attract you closer to your success. You want it to be something that pulls you in the direction of your goal. The more emotional you can make it, the stronger it will be.

One reason I wanted to create a better morning routine was because I wanted to be more productive. I wanted to get more done earlier in the day so I could spend more time with my family.

Another reason was because I wanted to reduce my stress. I found myself rushing and hurrying in the mornings, reacting to whatever came up. This was starting my day off on the wrong foot and spilling over into all the other areas of my life.

Create a reason that works for you. It will be extra motivation on those days when you do not feel like getting up. It will be the extra boost you need to create the habits you need to become a better version of yourself.

Answer these questions:

Review the following questions below and write down your answers. You will gain a lot of insight and understanding about yourself.

1. What benefits do you expect to gain from a morning routine?
2. How will a morning routine improve your life?
3. How will it affect your life if you continue your current morning routine?

The 4 Pillars of Morning Magic

It would be too simple to say a morning routine is only about the morning. From my experience, there are four main parts that you should be aware of. By being aware of each part, you can capitalize and improve each one by one.

The four pillars are:

- Night Time Rituals
- High-Quality Sleep
- Waking Up Productive
- Morning Magic

Each one plays a vital role and they are all interconnected. For instance, if you get poor sleep it may be difficult to wake up and will affect your morning routine. The things you do the day before can alter the next day. For instance, if you drink a lot of caffeine or alcohol, it can drastically affect the quality of your sleep and how you feel the next morning. This will affect your mood and your performance.

We will go into more detail about each one and point out some useful tips for maximizing each step along the way. One thing to remember is that they are all important and interconnected. Improving one of them can have positive effects in all areas.

Pillar #1: Night Time Rituals

What do you usually do each night leading up to sleep? It turns out that the things you do before sleep can play an important role in the quality and quantity of sleep you get each night.

Do you have a night time ritual? Chances are you do, but you may not be aware of it. Night time rituals are very similar to morning routines. You probably have similar habits you repeat nightly before bed. Think about a typical night. What do you do? What motions do you go through when preparing for bed?

For the next few days, start tracking your last 2-3 hours before you go to sleep. Be conscious of the activities you are doing and the amount of time you spend on each. Remember that being aware of your actions allows you to consciously choose what you do. So for the next few days, observe all your actions at night.

Use the "Night Time Ritual Tracking Chart" in the Morning Magic Starter Kit (www.levelupstar.com/morningmagic) to keep up with your activities. Track your behavior for a few days without any judgement. It is best to just witness your behavior and do things as you normally would to get a better understanding of your habits.

Why would I create a night time ritual?

After you track your night time behaviors for a few days, you will probably start to see a pattern. There is a correlation between your night time activities and the quality and quantity of sleep you get. Your quality of sleep affects your energy levels the next morning and day. In return this affects your day.

What we aim to do is improve each step of the Four Pillars, thereby setting you up for success each and every day. This is why we are starting with the basics. If you build a strong foundation, it will make everything else much easier and more effective.

Night time rituals can prime your body for sleep. It can prepare your body and mind for a good night's rest. Every person will be different, but you should consider picking and choosing from the list below to create your own night time ritual at least 30-60 minutes before bed. These ideas are only suggestions. You can create your own rituals based on your circumstances and preferences.

14 Night Time Ritual Ideas

Read over this list of night time ritual ideas. You can choose the ones that you like best and start implementing them into your routine.

1. Take a warm bath or shower

During sleep, your body temperature naturally dips. When you take a warm bath and soak in a tub, the warm water will cause your temperature to rise. When you get out, your body will rapidly cool down causing you to relax more. A warm shower can have the same effect but it is less effective compared to a bath.

2. Listen to relaxing music, podcast, or audiobook

Play some relaxing tunes and decompress. Listen to something that you enjoy or look forward to hearing. This will take your mind off the events of the day and allow you to relax and prepare for a good night's sleep ahead.

3. Dim the lights

Set the mood. How is your environment lit at night? Bright light exposure can stimulate parts of the brain that control hormones, your body temperature, and functions that can make you feel wide awake.

Particularly exposure to screens (phones, TV, and tablets) can have a negative effect on your sleep. In the hour or two before you get ready for bed, try to ditch the electronics. They emit blue light, and this can prevent or inhibit the release of melatonin (which reduces alertness and makes sleep enticing).

If you must use your electronic devices, consider using blue blocker glasses. These will block blue light from entering your eyes. Also consider setting the "night shift mode" on your devices. This will make the lights on your device less bright.

Lights can play a big factor into the mood or setting in your home. Use warm-colored lights with hues of reds or yellows (similar to sunset) in the evening and night. Warm glowing lights will be more relaxing and prime your body for sleep.

4. Read a book or magazine

While trying to avoid electronic screens, you can read a physical book or magazine. Read something that entertains you and allows you to "disconnect" for a while. Fiction books are a popular choice.

5. Journal about your day

Journaling is a great way to reduce stress, document your life, and organize your thoughts. You can recap your day and remind yourself of your daily wins. It is a nice way to end the day on a positive note and reflect on the good things in your life.

6. Prayer and meditation

Calm your mind. Take the focus off yourself. Decompress and relieve stress by focusing on others. Remind yourself of the blessings in your life. Pray for your loved ones.

Meditation is also a great way to calm your thoughts and relax. Most people think meditation is difficult or they do not know if they are doing it right. I recommend downloading the Headspace app (https://www.headspace.com) and going through the free training course, "Take 10". The meditations are guided so you will be led through the entire process. It is a great start for beginners. It is like a warm bath for your mind.

Omvana (http://www.omvana.com) is another great app for meditation, sleep, focus, and relaxation. There are lots of different types of meditations, affirmations, sound tracks, and relaxing sounds available to listen to.

7. Progressive muscle relaxation

You can use progressive muscle relaxation to relax your body. This can lower tension, decrease stress levels, and help you relax. If you are regularly tense, it is worth a try. You can find guided progressive muscle relaxations on Omvana, YouTube, or search for them online.

8. Focus on the breath

Breath is life. Your pattern of breathing can affect your state of consciousness. Try inhaling fully for 4-5 seconds. Hold the breath for three seconds and then release fully. Repeat five times. Focusing on the breath can instantly calm and relax you. This is especially useful when you are angered.

9. Visualization

We all use visualization daily even if you do not realize it. Do you ever daydream or play out scenarios in your mind? Can you recall a person's face or recall an event in your mind? This is visualization.

It turns out that you can use visualization to improve your performance or get better. Brain studies have revealed that thoughts produce the same mental activity as actions. In other words, you "practice" events in your mind and technically get better.

In an experiment by Australian psychologist Alan Richardson (Randolph, 2002), three random groups of people were chosen to shoot basketball free throws. The first group would practice daily for 20 days. The second group only shot free throws on day 1 and day 20. The third group did the same as the second group shooting free throws on day 1 and day 20 but there was one difference. Members of the third group were instructed to spend 20 minutes daily visualizing shooting free throws.

After 20 days, the group that practiced daily (the first group) improved 24%. The second group that did not practice at all did not improve any. The third group, which only practiced mentally, improved by 23%!

When visualizing, it is best to use as many senses as possible. "Feel" things around you. "Hear" noises associated with the actions. "See" it happen. See yourself being successful. You can use visualization to rehearse any event in your mind.

10. Affirmations

Affirmations can be a very powerful tool you can use to reprogram your subconscious mind. By affirming your intention, you are making a declaration to what you will or will not do.

We use affirmations all the time. Some work in our favor and some are working against us. Do you ever make a mistake and jokingly say, "I'm so stupid." Or have you ever heard someone affirm, "I'm always late." Even though these statements may not intentionally mean harm, they do create negative consequences. They are both affirming statements that are speaking to your subconscious mind in a negative way.

You can create your own affirmations that work in your favor. Affirmations can be used to prime you to be a morning person. I like to use two different sets of affirmations that help me go to sleep at night and to begin the day with power and enthusiasm.

In the Morning Magic Starter Kit (www.levelupstar.com/morningmagic), you can find my morning and night affirmations. There is also a template to create your own. I use the night affirmations as part of my night time ritual and the morning affirmations as part of my Morning Magic. The important thing is to recite your affirmations with emotion and envision yourself doing the things you are affirming. Recite the affirmations with power, enthusiasm, and emotion.

11. Prepare yourself for tomorrow

Make tomorrow morning as simple as possible. What can you do tonight that reduces the amount of decisions that you have to make in the morning? You could go ahead and fix your lunch. You could set out the clothes you are going to wear tomorrow. You could pack your bag in advance. You could set your gym clothes or running shoes beside the bed.

Think about things that will make your morning run a little smoother and take small actions to ensure the likelihood of your success with ease. This will reduce your stress and anxiety about being overwhelmed or rushed in the morning. Plus it will reduce your cognitive load and the number of decisions you have to make.

12. Cuddling

This may not come as a surprise, but cuddling has several scientifically proven benefits. For starters, it helps your body release oxytocin (feel good hormone). Cuddling can deepen your relationship, reduce stress, reduce anxiety, and make you happier. Makes you want to go cuddle, right?

13. Review your successes.

End your day by going over all the good things that happened to you during the day. Review all the positive things that happened and your wins. By ending the day on a good note, you are reinforcing the positive in your life. You are ending the day with a win.

This can improve your perspective on your life. By focusing on the good that is happening, you will start to find more of it in your life. Where focus goes, energy flows.

14. Make it fun.

Make this an enjoyable time that you can look forward to. Your night time rituals do not have to be exact. Mix and match things that you enjoy. You can experiment and try new things. Do activities that help you relax and feel good. The point is to make it a special time for you to wind down and prime your mind and body for sleep.

What relaxes you?

This list of ideas above is only suggestions. You know yourself the best, so it is up to you to choose things that fit your schedule, personality, and personal preference.

Create a schedule and stick to it (at least for a few days). Consistency is the key. You will have to train your body and mind. You can always change your schedule, but do it enough times to learn from it. If you decide to switch things up make sure you understand what you do and do not like about your current schedule.

Under no circumstances should you try to "wing it". We are humans. We forget things. We make mistakes. Create a plan. Eliminate the additional cognitive load of trying to remember what things you need to do and what order they need to be completed by using the "Night Time Ritual Checklist" in the Morning Magic Starter Kit.

Pillar #2: High-Quality Sleep

"A good laugh and a long sleep are the best cures in the doctor's book."

~ Irish Proverb

How much sleep do we really need? Sleep requirements depend on the person. There is no "one size fits all" answer. Some people can easily perform on six hours of sleep, while some people require 8-10 hours of sleep. According to a study by the National Sleep Foundation (Foundation, 2015), sleep requirements vary depending on the person and what stage of life they are in.

Newborns require 14-17 hours of sleep while older adults only require 7-8 hours of sleep. Research cannot pinpoint an exact number because there are multiple variables that play a factor in sleep requirements such as age, diet, lifestyle, light exposure, and more. Each person should pay attention to their own individual needs and listen to your own body. You know when you have had a good night's rest.

Sleep should rejuvenate and refresh you. Do you have to depend on caffeine in the morning? It may be a sign that you are not getting a good night's rest. Remember, awareness is the key. Review the questions below about your sleep patterns.

Answer these questions:

- How many hours of sleep do you get per night on average?
- On a scale of 1-10, how do you feel when you wake up?
- How much caffeine do you consume daily? What time of day?
- How many hours of sleep does it take to make you feel fully refreshed?
- What time do you normally get in bed?

The point of these questions is not to be judgmental or critical. Answer them honestly. It will help you become more aware about your patterns of behavior and uncover some habitual routines you might be unconsciously repeating.

Problems with Lack of Sleep

Sleep deprivation seems to be popular among Americans. According to the U.S. Center for Disease Control and Prevention (CDC, 2015), nearly 30% of American adults claim they are sleeping six hours or less per day.

So what's the problem with missing out on a little sleep? We have jobs, kids to take care of, and bills to pay. There's just not enough time in the day, right? Before I answer this question, let's address some of the side effects of sleep deprivation.

Sleep deprivation side effects:

- Kills sex drive
- Ages your skin
- Can cause depression
- Impairs judgement
- Can cause weight gain
- Increases likelihood of accidents
- Dumbs you down and increases forgetfulness
- Puts you at risk for heart attack, heart disease, high blood pressure, stroke, and diabetes to name a few

Not convinced yet?

To make matters even worse, 44% of night shift workers report getting less than six hours of sleep compared to 28% that work during the day. About 69% of warehouse and transportation workers and a little over 52% of healthcare and social assistance workers are not getting enough sleep either.

These are people we put lots of trust in, on the roads and in the hospital. This is literally a life and death situation. Sleep deprivation can be very dangerous and it puts those people at increased risk of injury along with those around them.

It is reported (NHTSA) that 20% of car crashes are linked to drowsiness behind the wheel. Also 4.7% of drivers reported nodding off or falling asleep while driving at least once in the past month. Do you want to share the road with sleeping drivers?

Why Should You Take Sleep Serious?

Besides wanting to avoid the negative effects of sleep deprivation, there are plenty of reasons why you should take sleep more serious. Sleep can work wonders for your body. It is a key factor in living a healthy life and feeling energetic.

Sleep has a huge factor on our overall well-being. It affects how we look, how we feel, how we perform, and our health. During sleep, our bodies repair muscles, release hormones that affect growth and appetite, consolidates memories, and rejuvenates the system.

Types of Sleep

There are two main types of sleep, rapid-eye-movement (REM) and non-rapid-eye-movement (NREM). REM sleep characterized by the rapid movement of the eyes during sleep. It is during REM sleep that most of your dreams occur. Interestingly, during REM sleep muscles in your arms and legs are temporarily paralyzed. This is believed to prevent the body from acting out dreams. When brain waves are measured on an EEG (electroencephalogram) during REM sleep, they were identified by a characteristic of low-amplitude, high frequency waves. These are small, fast waves that show patterns of high activity.

According to sleep research from Harvard Medical School (Harvard Medical School, 2007), NREM sleep has three stages (N1, N2, and N3). The stages start with N1 and progress as the brain waves become slower and more synchronized. The eyes continue to remain still, unlike in REM sleep. N3 is the deepest stage of NREM sleep and is referred to as "deep sleep".

Sleep follows patterns or cycles. Each cycle typically lasts 70 to 120 minutes. The first cycle is usually the longest. During these cycles your body progresses from N1 to N2 to N3 and then enters REM sleep.

N1 sleep is very short. It lasts anywhere from one to seven minutes. N2 sleep can last anywhere from 10 to 25 minutes. As N2 sleep progresses there is an increase in slow wave activity in the brain that is characteristic of N3 or deep sleep. As you enter N3, external stimuli have fewer effects on you and it becomes much more difficult to awaken a person from sleep.

After N3 stage sleep, movements of the body may cause a short period of ascension to N2, but it is quickly followed by REM sleep. A typical healthy adult will engage in REM sleep about 25% of total sleep.

These patterns continue to alternate cyclically throughout the night. Most NREM occurs early in the night and the length of REM sleep increases during the night. The cycle continues in stages throughout sleep.

How Do You View Sleep?

Your perspective on sleep can play a role in how seriously you take sleep. Do you view sleep as a waste of time or do you see it as an opportunity to rejuvenate and refresh? If you treat sleep as a waste of time, you will not seek to improve your sleep. After all, sleep is just as important as eating and breathing. If it is neglected, you are only harming yourself.

Try to be excited about sleep. View it as a refreshing part of the day. Your body is doing miraculous work to prepare yourself for tomorrow. This is a time of restoration. Memories are being consolidated, the body is repairing itself, and healing occurs. Your body is performing miracles as you sleep.

Wearables for Tracking Sleep

Before we get into the technical aspects of improving sleep, it is very important that you become aware of your sleep patterns. Do you have any idea the quality of sleep you are getting? You might have a clue based on how you feel the following morning, but are there any patterns emerging?

One recommendation is to start tracking your sleep with a tracker or app. This way you can quantify your sleep based. Once you track a few nights of sleep, you will gain a better understanding of your sleep, how long you sleep, and how many times you wake up during the night.

Here are a few devices and apps for tracking sleep. Some of the apps are free and some cost money. Do your own homework and research when deciding which one to choose. As of the writing of this book, these are the ones I found, but new technology is created daily. There will be many more available as time passes.

Sleep Tracking Devices

Up by Jawbone

Fitbit

Misfit

Food	Tryptophan [g/100 g of food]	Protein [g/100 g of food]	Tryptophan/Protein [%]
egg white, dried	1.00	81.10	1.23
spirulina, dried	0.93	57.47	1.62
cod, atlantic, dried	0.70	62.82	1.11
soybeans, raw	0.59	36.49	1.62
cheese, Parmesan	0.56	37.90	1.47
sesame seed	0.37	17.00	2.17
cheese, cheddar	0.32	24.90	1.29
sunflower seed	0.30	17.20	1.74
pork, chop	0.25	19.27	1.27
turkey	0.24	21.89	1.11
chicken	0.24	20.85	1.14
beef	0.23	20.13	1.12
oats	0.23	16.89	1.39
salmon	0.22	19.84	1.12
lamb, chop	0.21	18.33	1.17
perch, Atlantic	0.21	18.62	1.12
chickpeas, raw	0.19	19.30	0.96
egg	0.17	12.58	1.33
wheat flour, white	0.13	10.33	1.23
baking chocolate, unsweetened	0.13	12.9	1.23
milk	0.08	3.22	2.34
rice, white, medium-grain, cooked	0.028	2.38	1.18
quinoa, uncooked	0.167	14.12	1.2
quinoa, cooked	0.052	4.40	1.1
potatoes, russet	0.02	2.14	0.84
tamarind	0.018	2.80	0.64
banana	0.01	1.03	0.87

Source: Wikipedia

Ideally, you want to have something light before bed such as yogurt, banana, a cup of milk, almond butter on whole grain toast, eggs, or even cherries. All these will help induce sleep and promote a good night's rest.

Some people like to wind down their evening with a cup of tea to help induce sleep. If you drink tea before bed, go for herbal tea that does not contain caffeine. There are multiple "sleepy time" teas on the market that you can choose from. Some of the most popular ones are Chamomile, Peppermint, Lemon Balm, Valerian Root, and Lavender.

5. Supplements

Before you consider taking supplements for sleep, please consult with your doctor or physician. If you are sleeping poorly, it is important to look at your lifestyle first. There could be a root cause to your sleeping behavior. Although some people just have problems or conditions that affect their sleep. That is why it is important to first check with your doctor.

There are many supplements and sleep aids out there that are effective. I suggest you do your own homework and seek professional advice before experimenting or using any of them.

6. Sleeping Accessories

While bedding trumps the list, there are other sleep accessories that you can use to enhance your rest and sleep. Here are a few:

<u>Sleep mask</u> – This is a simpler and cheaper alternative to blackout curtains. A sleep mask basically blocks out the light allowing you to sleep in darkness. The only downfall with a sleep mask is that it is annoying to have something on your face all night, but they are effective.

<u>White noise machine</u> – White noise can buffer and muffle other disturbing sounds that can hinder your sleep. If you live in a noisy neighborhood, this can help big time.

<u>Earplugs</u> – Are you a light sleeper? Some people prefer no noise at all (me), but my wife likes white noise. If that is the case consider finding a good pair of earplugs to sleep in silence.

7. Eliminate Mind Chatter

Do you ever have problems going to sleep because of mind chatter? Nagging thoughts that are repeated over and over can really interrupt the sleep process. It could be anything from worry to thinking about what you have to do tomorrow. These ongoing and involuntary thoughts can keep you awake all night.

Here are a few ways to deal with these annoying thoughts:

<u>Journal</u> – Use a journal to reflect on your day and capture any wins or positive things that happened. End the day on a good note remembering the key moments of the day. If you are in a foul mood, release your thoughts on paper. It is symbolic for getting those thoughts out of your mind and capturing them on paper. If you want to go one step further, do as Chuck Norris does. After he captures the negative

thoughts on paper, he destroys the paper and with the paper his negative thoughts are also destroyed.

Focus on the breath – Focus on your breathing. Inhale deeply and exhale fully. Focus on the point in between breaths where the inhale becomes the exhale and vice versa. Focus on counting your breaths to 10 and starting over when you reach 10. If you find yourself distracted just pick up where you left off. By focusing on the breath and counting, you will completely take your mind off the other thoughts that were racing through your head before. There are many breathing apps you can download and use from your smartphone.

Top 10 Things to Avoid Before Bed

1. Screens (Phones, TV, Tablets, Electronics)

The blue light emitted from these devices will disrupt production of melatonin in your body. If you absolutely must use a device, consider wearing blue blocker glasses to block the blue light from hitting your eyes. You can also set most phones in a "night shift" that dims the light and gives it a warmer glow. For laptops and desktops, you can download f.lux (https://justgetflux.com) for free. It basically makes your screen display adapt the color to the time of day. It will make the colors warmer at night to avoid blue light emission.

2. Large Meals

Eating too much before bed can make you feel bloated and full. Avoid being uncomfortable by eating a lighter meal that is easier to digest.

3. Alcohol

Booze will make you feel drowsy but it comes at a price. It will reduce the amount of REM sleep you get. Try to lay off the drinks about two to three hours before bed.

4. Caffeine

Anything that contains caffeine will stimulate your body and make falling asleep more difficult. Try to avoid caffeine after at least six hours before bed.

5. Too Much Water

Hydration is important but drinking too much before bed can cause you to wake up during the night to use the restroom.

6. Nicotine

Besides all the other negative health benefits of smoking and nicotine use, it can also hinder your sleep. Nicotine is a stimulant and can make falling asleep difficult.

7. Worry

Lots of restless nights have been created by worry. If something is bothering you try to find a way to resolve it before bed. If it is completely out of your control, focus on the things you can control (thoughts, words, and actions).

8. Arguments

Fighting can elevate cortisol and other stress hormones that will make falling asleep more difficult. Resolve arguments when possible.

9. Work Related Tasks

Thinking about work and the tasks you have to do the next day are recipes for a restless night. Everything has its own place and time.

10. Email or Text

Try to avoid starting conversations later in the night. When you are trying to sleep and your phone starts vibrating or buzzing it can be a distraction. The anticipation of waiting for a reply can make falling asleep seem impossible at times.

Pillar #3: Waking Up Productive

"Once you wake up and smell the coffee, it's hard to go back to sleep."

–Fran Drescher

The alarm is going off and it would feel so good to hit the snooze button just one more time. That eluding sleep you want so badly has come to an end. Now it is time to get up and do grown-up stuff.

Withings ran a sleep study (Withings, 2014) and concluded that 57% of Americans snooze. Also 58% of Americans admit to staying in bed more than five minutes every morning. Let's do some quick math. Let's say you snooze an extra 10 minutes a day. That does not seem like much, right?

- 10 minutes per day x 7 days per week = 70 minutes per week
- 10 minutes per day x 30 days = 300 minutes (5 hours) per month
- 10 minutes per day x 365 days = 3,650 minutes (60.8 hours) per year
- 60.8 hours = 2.5 days per year

Just by snoozing 10 minutes per day, you will spend 2.5 days in a year snoozing. I know in the past I have been guilty of this. To be honest, I would sometimes snooze 4-5 times. That equals 10-12 days a year of snoozing! When it is put in that perspective, it totally changes the value of a few extra minutes of low quality sleep.

Every time you snooze, you are procrastinating the start of the day. If you hate getting up in the morning, snoozing only makes you repeat the action you "think" you hate.

The Withings study also concluded that only 33% of Americans defined their wake up experience as "good". Over two-thirds of Americans are not happy with their morning experience. **So how can we make waking up enjoyable?**

There are a few things to think about. What are you using to wake you? What do you have planned when you wake up? Are there any preventative measures to stop you from going back to sleep?

Here is a list of things you can start implementing to make waking up much easier.

11 Productive Wake Up Strategies

1. Gradual Timing

Your body can get used to waking up earlier. For many people, they decide a time and try to start waking up much earlier than they normally do. This often leads to failure, because the body is not acclimated to it yet.

Let's say you normally wake up at 7:00 AM and you want to start waking up at 5:00 AM. Instead of setting your alarm for 5:00 AM and dreading that wake up time, what if you started waking up 15 minutes earlier than normal for a few days.

You would wake up at 6:45 instead of 7:00. After a few days of this you would start waking up at 6:30. Continue this for a few days and then start waking up at 6:15. Gradually work your way down to 5:00 AM without making it unbearable. Your body will gradually adapt to it without being overwhelmed and you will barely notice the change.

I have been testing this for several weeks. The results are amazing. I am now waking up two hours earlier without the resistance or overload to drastically changing my wake up time.

2. Change Your Alarm Tone

I think it would be fair to say that most of us HATE our alarm tone. For as long as I can remember, my alarm was the preset generic tone on my phone or alarm clock. It was that obnoxious noise that made waking up feel painful. You could call this a "rude awakening".

Can a bad wake up experience affect your day? Sure, if you let it. What would happen if you changed your alarm tone to something refreshing? What if you changed your alarm tone to one of your favorite songs?

Think about how you are waking up. If it is not enjoyable and delightful, you can bet it will feel painful. Consider changing the tone of your alarm to something that makes you feel happy and energized. After all, it is the first thing you hear to start the day.

3. Get Up Immediately

One of the reasons we snooze is because it is so easy to lay there. If your alarm clock or phone is right beside you, it is really simple to hit snooze and roll over without even thinking about it. Here is a game changing idea. **Put your alarm clock or phone on the other side of the room so you are forced to get up on your feet to turn it off.**

This will mean you have to actually get out of bed. Once you are out of bed, the hard part is over. You are on your feet and moving. This is an instant jolt of momentum. Just keep moving and start your day.

Do not rationalize or negotiate with yourself. Once you are up, stay up.

4. Wake Up Your Senses

You have been asleep for several hours. You might still feel groggy when you wake up. Splash cold water on your face or take a cold shower. This will wake you up immediately. Cold water will activate sensors under your skin, slightly increase heart rate, and create an adrenaline rush to wake you up.

5. Get in the Light

Expose yourself to bright lights, particularly sunlight if possible. Our bodies essentially run on a clock called the circadian rhythm. It is a 24-hour cycle that responds to light and darkness in our environments. This is true for most living things.

Circadian rhythms are affected by the signals from our environment (light). The circadian rhythm has influence over your sleep-wake cycle, body temperature, hormone release, and other functions of the body. Light will tell your body to wake up. This is also why you want to avoid bright lights at night.

Sunlight exposure is also one of the best sources for Vitamin D. It can also improve your mood. The good news is that all you really need is about 10 minutes of exposure to get the benefits of it.

6. Get Your Blood Flowing

Do some type of physical activity as soon as you get out of bed that will get your blood flowing. You could do push-ups, sit-ups, jumping jacks, stretch, or go for a run. This will increase your alertness and make you feel more energetic.

Exercise can also improve your mood. Endorphins (feel good hormones) are released during exercise. Not only that, regular exercise can reduce stress, boost esteem, improve sleep, strengthen your heart, lower blood pressure, strengthen muscles, reduce body fat, and make you look and feel great!

7. Drink Water

You have not had anything to drink for a couple of hours. Your body is partially dehydrated after a long sleep. It is time to replenish your tissues and cells. Drink at least 8-16 ounces of water to clean out your system.

Drinking water first thing in the morning has lots of benefits. It will fire up your metabolism, keep you regular, flush out toxins, and refresh your body.

8. Eliminate Choices

Make mornings as simple as possible. Eliminate as many choices or decisions as you can. Can you set the coffee pot on an automatic timer? Can you make your breakfast the night before? How about deciding what you will wear in advance? Put your running shoes or gym clothes beside the bed. If you can eliminate choices or reduce the amount of steps in doing something, it will make your mornings run much smoother.

9. Accountability Partner

Find someone that will hold you accountable for waking up on time every day. It is easy to let yourself off the hook and snooze when no one is watching. What if you had to report to someone else via text, phone call, or email first thing in the morning?

Accountability partners are AMAZING. You can find out more about accountability partners later in the book under the chapter, *8 Powerful Tips to Make it Stick.*

10. Rewards

Create small incentives for waking up immediately. This can be anything from your favorite cup of coffee to a small snack or treat. Create a reward system that gives you incentives for complying to a quick morning start.

Always remember, what gets rewarded gets repeated. Even if the reward or incentive is very small, it does not matter. If you want behavior to be repeated, create an incentive or reward that praises the behavior you want repeated.

11. Get Excited Like a Kid on Christmas

You know what I am talking about. Watch any child the night before Christmas. They are so excited to get up as early as possible in the morning. It does not matter how much sleep they get either. They are so enthusiastic about the morning.

Now think about yourself. What excites you like this? There has to be something you really look forward to. Can you start doing that first thing in the morning? This will help link massive pleasure to waking up and beginning the day with power and enthusiasm.

Pillar #4: Morning Magic

Abra cadabra! You have come a long way and now it is time for the magic. You have gotten plenty of high-quality sleep. You have had no problem waking up earlier than normal, and now you are wide awake and out of bed. So what's next?

Now it is time to decide what you will be doing after you get up. There is no need to be waking up earlier if you do not have anything planned. This will be a specific amount of time that is dedicated to YOU. You will use this time to feed your mind, body, and soul.

You can use this time to work on any area of your life. This will be up to you to decide where you want to put your focus. The amazing thing is that if there is any areas of your life that you are unhappy with, you have the power to work on them and change it for the better.

Here are areas you could focus on:

- Health and diet
- Fitness and exercise
- Money and finances
- Goals and intentions
- Family and home

- Relationships
- Hobbies
- Personal improvement
- Learning and education
- Job and career
- Spirituality and prayer

Step 1: Decide how much time you want to dedicate to your plan.

This is your plan, so you get to call the shots. How much time do you want to dedicate to your morning routine? Every person will vary. Basically, you are going to focus only on the things you want to do. Nothing else can interfere. Some people like to spend 15, 30, 45, or 60 minutes for their routines. You decide how much time you want to spend and how you will use it.

Here's something else to think about. Remember when we talked about my snoozing habit and how much time it took from me per year? What if you dedicated 10 minutes here and 10 minutes there to level-up yourself each day? Over the course of a year, you could have profound results. It does not take much, but consistently over time you will see big results.

Example: Let's say you wanted to work on your body, learning, and meditation. What if you gave each one 10 minutes of time per category each morning? That's only 30 minutes per day. What kind of results would it create in your life after six months? One year?

Step 2: Decide what areas you want spend your time on.

Get an idea of what kind of activities you want to dedicate yourself to in the morning. I personally like to spend part of my morning routine writing. The reason is because everyone is asleep and the house is still quiet.

In the past, I liked to go to the gym or run early in the morning. You may want to spend this time reading, studying, meditating, or exercising. You can switch things up. Just have an idea of what areas you want to work on in the morning. We will get to the finer details in the next chapter.

Step 3: Get a clear mental picture of your perfect morning.

If everything were perfect, how would your ideal morning flow? You must envision it before it can happen. Become acquainted with the fine details in your mind. How does the morning go? What do you do first? What follows that? How do you wrap things up? Do you wake up energetic and enthused? Do you want to eat first? Maybe you want to immediately go for a jog or jump in the shower.

Think about every little detail. What would be the best possible outcome? There is no reason that you cannot make it happen. How you start your day can dictate the mood for the rest of the day. You might as well do it on your terms.

Step 4: Write down every detail.

Take your clear mental picture of your perfect morning and put it on paper. Include every little detail. I cannot explain it, but there is something very special about turning your thoughts into words. It is the first manifestation of your thought. It is the first sign of life of the things you were thinking.

Jot down everything that comes to mind. This will be a blueprint for your perfect morning! You will use this blueprint to actually put together your Morning Magic.

Samples of Morning Routines

It seems that throughout history that some of the most successful people have been early risers. Just waking up early does not and will not make you successful. It is what you do with your time that makes a difference.

No matter whom you are, where you are from, or what your circumstances are, we all have the same amount of time each day. Each day is comprised of 1,440 minutes. What you do with those minutes determines your level of success. Therefore this book is not about time management, but rather it is about self-management. You cannot control time, it is fixed. But you do control your efforts and what you do with your time.

You do not have to create some elaborate system. Simplicity is the key.

My Morning Routine

My plan is still a work in progress. Every now and then I change it up depending on the time of the year and what I have going on. For instance, when I am training for a marathon I might be running in the morning. As of the writing of this book, this is how my morning routine is going.

5:45 – Wake up immediately and do pushups

5:50 – Drink 20 ounces of water

5:55 - Morning shake and coffee while listening to podcast/audiobook

6:20 – Spend time with my family while they have breakfast

7:00 – Journal

7:10 – Write for 30 minutes (book or blog)

7:40 – Meditate with the Headspace app

7:55 – Affirmations and visualize my perfect day

8:00 – Start my work day

There is nothing complicated about this. I simply do a few things that I think are important in my life to start the day and it gives me a level-up boost. These are the areas I cover:

- Body/Fitness
- Nutrition
- Family
- Journal (gratitude, priorities for day, reflection)
- Mind
- Affirmations/Intentions
- Career

This is completely flexible too. I usually give my morning routine a few days for a trial run. That way I can see how it flows and figure out ways to make it run smoother.

Every week during my weekly review, I go over the process and see what is working and what does not fit. If I am having resistance to a particular part of the routine I try to figure out why and what I can do to fix it, change it, or eliminate it.

You will want to keep experimenting and changing things up until you find a routine that feels right. Sometimes just changing the order of things can make a big difference. The reason I do pushups immediately when waking up is to get my blood flowing and make me feel more awake. The reason I do affirmations and visualization last is because I like to affirm what I am going to do for the day and then see it happening in my mind. A few months ago I was doing affirmations first thing after I woke up. It just did not click. I needed something to make me feel more awake. After some experimentation and switching things up, I found a better solution.

Start the Day with Success

A morning routine will give you confidence and energy because you are doing meaningful things before most people even wake up. This will give you a sense of accomplishment and pride. Plus you are becoming a better version of yourself.

This builds momentum and spills into the rest of your day. Remember earlier in the book when we discussed how you start your day can determine the day itself? What if you started every single day on your terms with success, power, and enthusasm? Sure that would be great, but think about the long term implications of this. No longer do you have to settle for what life throws at you.

A few days of this would create a fantastic week. A few weeks of this would make an amazing month. A few months of this would create the best year of your life. It all comes back to the small things. Instead of snoozing 20 minutes a day, you can use that time to create your life the way you want it. You do not have to do anything huge or monumental. All it takes is a few small tweaks. Small hinges swing big doors.

What is Success to You?

Before you create your morning routine it is important to define success. What is success to you? What are your intentions with this morning routine? If you know what your target is you will increase the likelihood of hitting the bullseye.

By knowing what will be a successful morning routine, you can create it exactly how you want it. This is a good time to look over your "perfect morning" that you wrote down earlier. When you start, things may not go as planned. That is why experimentation will be important. If things are not perfect, that is ok! Success is not being perfect.

Success is the accomplishment of an aim or purpose. If your aim is to improve your life and become a better version of yourself, then a morning routine will create success for you. Incremental growth and improvement can lead to massive gains over time.

Creating Your Morning Magic

"There is a real magic in enthusiasm. It spells the difference between mediocrity and accomplishment."

–Norman Vincent Peale

Now it is time to create your Morning Magic. This will be the plan you create for yourself to do when you wake up in the morning. This will be a special time designated for YOU. Before we begin, be sure to answer these questions:

1. How much time are you going to dedicate to your Morning Magic?
2. What areas of your life are you going to work on?
3. What activities are you going to do?
4. What order are you going to do them?
5. How much time are you going to give to each area?

Chart Your Morning

We want to make things as simple as possible to start with. The simpler the plan is the higher the likelihood that you will follow through and be successful.

Use the "Create Your Own Morning Magic" chart found in the Morning Magic Starter Kit (www.levelupstar.com/morningmagic) to fill in your morning routine. You can schedule the activities, the time, and how long each will last.

What I like to do when first starting is to set a timer for each. Let's say I am going to spend 60 minutes on my Morning Magic and I am going to do these four activities: fitness, meditation, journaling, and affirmations. I would set up my chart like this:

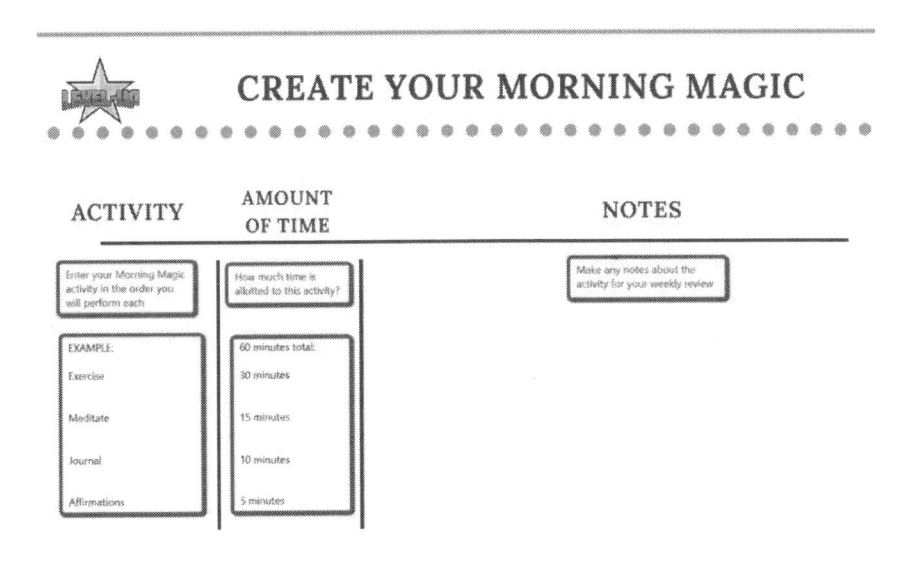

CREATE YOUR MORNING MAGIC

ACTIVITY	AMOUNT OF TIME	NOTES
Enter your Morning Magic activity in the order you will perform each	How much time is allotted to this activity?	Make any notes about the activity for your weekly review
EXAMPLE:	60 minutes total:	
Exercise	30 minutes	
Meditate	15 minutes	
Journal	10 minutes	
Affirmations	5 minutes	

Some activities will not require as much time as others. For instance, it only takes me a few minutes to recite my affirmations. You probably would not want to allot as much time for that as you do your workout. You will have to figure out your own timing through experimentation.

Here are some popular time amounts people have been using for their Morning Magic:

Power Hour – This is an entire hour packed with powerful morning routines that energize and get your mind, body, and spirit ready for the day!

45 To Feel Alive – This is 45 minutes to start your day with power and enthusiasm!

Terrific 30 – This is 30 minutes in which you dedicate to yourself. The terrific 30 is perfect for those with a busy schedule.

15 Minute Jumpstart – This is for those that do not have a lot of time to spare. This is a great start for beginners. You can always work your way up.

50+ Morning Activity Ideas

Still not sure what you want to do for your morning routine and need some ideas to begin? You can pick and choose from the list below. You can modify anything on the list to fit your needs. I have broken the idea list down into categories for your convenience.

Fitness/Health

- Exercise (weights or no weight)
- Walk the dog
- Running
- Biking
- Yoga
- Stretching
- Drink a glass of water
- Morning smoothie or shake
- Healthy breakfast

Mind/Relaxation

- Meditation
- Prayer
- Silence
- Journal

- Sit and enjoy
- Read
- Visualization
- List things you are grateful for
- Watch/listen to something inspiring

Family/Relationships

- Have breakfast with family
- Say "I love you" to someone
- Send an uplifting text or email
- Call a friend or family member
- Write a letter to someone
- Hug a loved one
- Kiss your spouse/partner

Change Your State

- Smile in the mirror for 30 seconds
- Do "power poses"
- Breathing exercises
- Listen to uplifting music
- Laugh - watch or listen to comedy
- Movement or dance

Personal

- Shower
- Personal grooming
- Hobbies
- Create to-do lists
- Prioritize events
- Plan the day ahead

Learning/Education

- Read
- Listen to podcast
- Listen to audiobook
- Learn a new skill
- Practice
- Study

Affirmations/Intentions

- Say affirmations
- Set intentions for the day
- Recite goals
- Review your progress
- Visualize your perfect day

Other

- Create something
- Tidy up
- Make up bed
- Go outside and get some fresh air
- See the sunrise
- Write a blog
- Paint or draw
- Sing
- Dance
- Write

Top 10 Things to Avoid in the Morning

Here is a list of the top 10 things to avoid each morning. These are things that will slow down your progress and hinder your results.

1. Snoozing

Create a "no snooze policy" and stick to it. Just remember that snoozing is procrastinating the start of your day.

2. Heavy breakfast

Eat a light breakfast. A heavy meal can make you feel bloated and uncomfortable.

3. Email

Avoid email if possible. Typically email can wait until later in the day. Those nagging emails usually steal your attention, time, and focus.

4. TV

Not all TV is bad, but your mornings should be dedicated to your own personal growth. Avoid the TV stealing your precious time.

5. Morning news

Most of the news is negative. Avoid feeding your mind negative news to start your day.

6. Multitasking

It is very difficult to do two things at a time and do them both in an excellent fashion. Focus on one thing at a time and give it your full attention. Only move on to the next task when the first task is complete.

7. Worry

How you start your day can dictate the entire day. Avoid worry if possible. Focus on the things you can control.

8. Arguments

Arguing is usually a battle of egos. Be the bigger person and let petty things go. You do not have to be right about everything. Arguments can get under your skin and affect you all day long if you let it.

9. Negative people

Avoid negative people. They have a tendency to rub off on others. Surround yourself with uplifting people that will support you.

10. Other distractions

There are a million other distractions that can steal your time and attention. Everyone has their own set of them. Your mornings are your personal time to give to yourself. Take advantage of your special time.

Stick-to-it-ness

The key is to make your plan stick. You want to make it run as smooth as possible and become a habit. How can you do this?

First, you must have a plan. Hopefully, you have taken the time to create your step-by-step plan for your own Morning Magic. Post your plan where you can see it daily.

Second, you must know your priorities. There will be days when things do not go according to plan. It is inevitable. What will you do on these days? If you know your priorities, you can make sure you do the most important things first. Whichever activities have the highest value to you, do them as soon as possible.

Build upon your success. The more you do this, the easier it will get. Celebrate small wins and build your momentum. There is no need to dwell on failures. Focus on what you can control and keep moving forward. Eventually you will be the master of your morning and you will be starting each and every day the way you designed it!

Focus on YOU. I know this sounds a little selfish, but this is your life we are talking about. Even if you are only spending

15 minutes each morning to do this, it is still a piece of time you can invest in yourself. The greatest investment you can ever make in your life is in yourself. It can produce the highest return on investment. If you want your life to be better, you have to get better. It all starts with YOU.

8 Powerful Tips to Make it Stick

Here are a few powerful tips to help you ensure that you follow through with your morning plan. You can use some of them or all of them. The more you use, the higher likelihood are your chances of success.

1. Accountability

Accountability partners are one of the most powerful ways to accomplish a goal. If you tell someone you are going to do something, you do not want to let them down. They can also be someone you have to report to, someone that provides feedback, and someone that can identify your strengths and weaknesses.

It is imperative that you find someone that will be stern, honest, and fair. It would be counterintuitive to choose someone that will allow you to slip up and quit. Accountability partners hold you responsible for what you say you are going to do.

Create Consequences

It turns out that we, as humans, will do more to avoid losing something than to gain something of equal value. This can be used to our advantage in these circumstances. Put something on the line with your accountability partner. Be very clear and precise about the stipulations.

For instance, give your partner $100 and tell him that he can keep it if you do not send him a picture of yourself out of bed every single morning before 5:30 AM for 30 straight days.

Why does this work? There are quite a few reasons. You will not want to let your accountability partner down. You will want to complete what you said you would complete. You will not want to lose your money due to your own laziness.

If you go about this alone there will be no one there to keep hold you responsible but yourself. It will make it easy to miss a day or let things slide a time or two. Accountability will accelerate your performance and help you stay on track. It also keeps you engaged in the process. It creates another reason why you are doing this. It also helps you measure your progress and success.

Social Media

Get on your favorite social media site and let everyone know what you intend to do. You can check in daily with a post or a tweet. Not only will you get lots of support, you will also get an added bonus of accountability. Once people start cheering you on and supporting you, it will be very hard to quit because you do not want to let them down!

Not only that, but you will also want to avoid the embarrassment associated with quitting. When you announce it to the world it is like burning the bridges. You will want to follow through with what you said.

Use the hashtag **#MorningMagic** on your posts. I would love to see what your morning routines are!

Get a Friend to Join You

Going about this by yourself can be difficult and lonely. Find a friend or family member to go through the challenge with you. You can share your experiences with each other, uplift one another when times get hard, and give each other feedback and advice. The journey will be a lot easier when you know someone else is going through the exact same thing as you are.

Contracts

Create a contract about your intentions and goals for your morning routine. Sign it and have someone else sign it. This is a symbolic form of accountability. Hang your contract where you will see it daily. This will remind you of your obligation to follow through.

2. Start Small

One big mistake that can be detrimental to your success is taking on too much too quickly. Start small and work your way up. If you are not accustomed with waking up earlier then adding too much to your plate will deplete your willpower quickly.

Pick one to three things you want to implement in your morning routine. Choose things that you consider to be simple but important to you. This will build your momentum and create small wins.

After a few days or weeks of success, you can start to add additional things one by one to your Morning Magic. The key is to get the hang of it and make it very doable without creating too much chaos in your mornings. Once you can easily go through your morning routine without any hiccups, then you can start adding more to it.

3. Simplicity

Simplicity is beautiful. For some reason our society believes that complexity is synonymous for value. This could not be further from the truth. Find simplicity in anything you do.

Can you reduce the number of steps it takes to do something? Can you make it fail proof? Can you make it simpler than it already is? These are the types of questions you can ask yourself when you review your progress each week.

Simplicity is the way.

4. Small Wins

Simplicity creates wins. Wins build momentum and confidence. Find ways to start the day with a number of small wins.

Remember, this does not have to be all or nothing. You can be creative and find ways to be simple and start small. You will start to link a sense of pleasure to your morning routine and look forward to it.

What gets rewarded gets repeated. Reward yourself for your wins.

5. Identify Threats or Obstacles

Look for threats or obstacles that may prevent you from success. Write them down and identify them. Think of everything you could possibly think of that would hinder your progress. Also identify ways you would handle it if it were to come up.

By being prepared in advance, you will know exactly what to do if and when something like that occurs. Most people are blindsided when adversity comes and they revert back to their old habits. Do not let this happen to you. Be proactive and decide the best choice of action for yourself.

6. Track Your Progress

Tracking your results is a form of accountability to yourself. You will be able to see what is getting completed and what is falling short of the mark. This is a great way to see patterns or problems with your order or timing.

Keep notes on what is working and what does not work. When you identify things that do not work you can overcome them by changing or planning a new way. Look for solutions.

7. Repetition is the Mother of all Skill

Keep going. Keep trying. The more you do something the better you become at it. If you fail, who cares? Keep trying. The more times you do something, the more acclimated you become with it. You will become more comfortable doing it. Your skill level will increase. You will get better at it. If something seems difficult at first, keep trying. Just know that you are making it easier as you go. It will not be instant, but it will become easier.

This is especially true for waking up in the morning at an earlier time. You do this at least once a year. When daylights savings time occurs in the spring, the clocks move forward one hour. The first few days are a little difficult to get adjusted to, but after a week or two it seems normal and you easily get used to it.

8. Divide into Segments or Rooms

Instead of viewing your entire morning routine as a whole, can you divide it into segments? This is part of the "divide and conquer strategy". You take a whole and divide it into quarters. This makes the tasks easier and more manageable.

You can also break your routine down according to rooms. For instance, kitchen, living room, and office. Each room has its own set of routines you do in the morning.

Wake up, have breakfast in the kitchen and read. Go in the living room and do exercises and stretch. Then end your morning routine in the office where you write in your journal.

You can be really creative and divide your routine into segments or rooms and make it much more manageable and doable.

Review, Tweak, Modify

"Without struggle there can be no progress."

– Frederick Douglas

Through each step on your way to create the perfect morning routine, you will want to review your progress. This will allow you to tweak and modify things so that they can run more effective and efficiently.

Anytime I undertake something new, I like to review my progress weekly. This allows me to give it enough time to gather results and create some progress. Each week I will review that progress and see where I am at compared to a few days ago. From there I can adjust and act accordingly.

Keep Score

Tracking your progress is very important. It will give you more insight to things that are working or not working. By having the results in front of you, it gives you the information needed to make future decisions.

Charts

There are a number of ways that you can track your progress. It all depends on what you are tracking and your preference. I personally like to track morning routines and habits on a piece of paper. I created the habit creation chart (www.levelupstar.com/resources) to do just that.

Basically it allows you to create new habits and behaviors for certain parts of the day. Each day that I perform that task, I put an X on that day for that task. This allows me to see what days I did my tasks, if I am missing days, and what patterns emerge. I usually follow through with it for at least a week before changing things up. After a week, I have enough data to decide if I need to keep doing it, change it, or try something new.

Apps

There are tons of apps out there that will allow you to track your habits or activities. I am old-school and use a piece of paper but some people find it easier to just use their smartphone. You can use apps like Evernote, Momentum, Habitca, HabitClock, Streaks, or find one that suits your needs. There are countless apps to choose from.

Mark the Calendar

This is another old-school tactic that I like to use. It is really handy if you keep your calendar where you see it often. My calendar is hanging right beside my computer screen so I literally see it dozens of times a day.

Once you start a streak or chain of X's on your calendar it can become addictive. You will not want to end the streak!

Weekly Review

Choose a day each week to review your progress and results. I typically do my review on Sunday afternoon. This allows me plan the week based on my results.

Your review will be based on your performance over the past seven days. This is why tracking is important, so you will have some data and results to review. Look over anything you have been tracking for the past few days and gather the evidence needed to answer these questions below. It is very important that you are honest during review. It is ok if you fall short of your goals or intentions. It is imperative that you learn from your mistakes and make corrections based on what happened and adjust accordingly.

There are four things you need to address during your review:

1. What were my results?
2. What went right? What were my successes?
3. What went wrong? Why?
4. Based on this information, what are my future actions?

Tweak and Modify

Use the information from the questions you answered on your weekly review to tweak and modify your plans for the following week. If things did not go according to plan, find out what was the root cause.

Throughout my experimentation, I have used the weekly review to learn so much about myself. When trying to implement new habits, it can be a little challenging at first. If you use your experiences as a learning process, it can dramatically increase the speed in which you achieve your goals. Failure is not a bad thing. It can be very helpful and insightful.

Sometimes things will not go as smoothly as you would like. If this happens, identify what is going on. The first thing you may want to try is a different order. Are things flowing well?

Could they flow better in a different order? Switch things up a little and see if that helps.

Perhaps what you are doing just does not work for you. Try new things. It is completely fine to try different things to see what you like the best. This is your morning routine. This is your life. The whole point of it is to increase YOUR happiness, well-being, and productivity.

Be flexible and open to change. When you identify things that are working well, figure out why. Results do not lie. Look over your weekly review and identify the things that went well, and do more of those types of things. Identify why it went well and see if you can implement that understanding into things that are not going as well.

Experiment

In everything you do, you will not be perfect. Do not expect to start out and things always go according to plan. Learn from your experiences and try new things in different orders. All of this is one big experiment.

You have to try multiple things to see what you like best. You have to fail to make progress. You have to keep trying. It is all one big learning game. Learn from everything that you do and keep running experiments. Eventually you will figure out the secret recipe for your success!

Putting Everything Together

Now it is time to put everything together and implement your Morning Magic! You have created a night time ritual that relaxes you before bed, you know how to get an amazing night's rest, you know how to wake up with power and enthusiasm, and you have created your Morning Magic. You are ready to go!

The rest is up to you. It all begins with a decision. Something special happens when a person makes a decision. That is usually the starting point for success. You know deep down in your heart that you are capable of amazing things. You have inside you the power to do more, be more, and have more in your life. Now it is time to get out there and make it happen!

I want to see you succeed. Be sure to download your Morning Magic Starter Kit (www.levelupstar.com/morningmagic) with all the tools you will need to help you along the way. You can also post pictures of your Morning Magic routine by using the hashtag **#MorningMagic**. Share your experiences with the world and inspire us to level-up our game!

Moving Forward

Well if you have made it this far, you should be really proud of yourself. You are the type of person that claims responsibility for your life and takes action. Unfortunately, this is the rare few. I applaud you for this.

Sometimes I wonder what the world would be like if there were more people like you. There is no doubt that it would create a massive positive impact in every area. That is one of the main reasons why I enjoy creating content like this. Even if it only affects a small percentage of people, I feel happy knowing it can help someone on a positive note.

The same goes for you. If you found any valuable insights in this book, *please share them with a friend of a loved one.* You never know the impact you can have on someone else's life by sharing one thought or idea. It could completely change their life for the better.

That was the case for me. It all started with one book that was recommended to me and it completely changed the course of my life. Knowledge is power, but only when you act upon it.

It has been an honor and a privilege writing this book for you. If there is anything I can help you out with or if you would like to say hello, please send me an email at *arrmon@levelupstar.com*. I really enjoy meeting like-minded people and making new friends. Feel free to reach out to me at any time! I hope to hear from you soon.

I wish you the very best and hope your mornings are early and bright!

Your friend,

Arrmon

Would You Like to Know More?

I have lots of other information that can help you level-up your life in multiple areas. If you would like instant notifications about new content, free or discounted book promotions, and more, just subscribe to my email list.

When I release new books, I like to run special promotions just for people on the list (usually $0.99 or sometimes free).

You will also get the *"Level-Up Power Guide"* for free! Check out the link below.

www.levelupstar.com/freegift

About the Author

Arrmon Abedikichi is the creator of the popular blog, www.levelupstar.com. It is a personal development blog dedicated to finding easy and practical ways to become a better version of yourself.

For many years Arrmon lived an ordinary life. After a tragic house fire where he lost everything, he decided to make a change. No longer could he live a life where he settled for "good enough". It was time to level-up his life in all areas.

In his blog, he shares his crazy experiments and adventures. Anyone looking for practical ways to level-up their life, this is a must read. It does not matter what category of your life it is. He covers focus, goals, time management, health, fun, lifestyle, philosophy, relationships, stress, adventure, video games, sports, and a lot more. He always puts a unique twist on things and keeps it simple and easy to understand.

Arrmon is a father of two, a loving husband, a life scientist, and a runner. He enjoys video games, sports, learning, exploring, and creating. Feel free to reach out to him any time at arrmon@levelupstar.com with questions, comments, or just to say hi!

Bibliography

(n.d.). Retrieved July 2016, from NHTSA: http://www.nhtsa.gov/people/injury/drowsy_driving1/Drowsy.html#NCSDR/NHTSA

CDC. (2015, September 3). Retrieved July 2016, from Centers for Disease Control and Prevention: http://www.cdc.gov/features/dssleep/

Foundation, N. S. (2015). National Sleep Foundation's Sleep Time Duration Recommendations: Methodology and Results Summary. *Sleep Health Journal*, 40-43.

Harvard Medical School. (2007, December 18). Retrieved July 2016, from Healthysleep.med.harvard.edu: http://healthysleep.med.harvard.edu/healthy/science/what/sleep-patterns-rem-nrem

Nielsen. (2014, December 3). *Nielsen News*. Retrieved June 2016, from Nielsen: http://www.nielsen.com/us/en/insights/news/2014/content-is-king-but-viewing-habits-vary-by-demographic.html

Randolph, K. (2002, May 15). *Sports Visualizations*. Retrieved July 2016, from Llewellyn: http://www.llewellyn.com/encyclopedia/article/244

Smith, K. S., & Ann, G. M. (2016, March 18). Retrieved June 2016, from NCBI: https://www.ncbi.nlm.nih.gov/pmc/articles/PMC4826769/

Withings. (2014, August 25). Retrieved July 2016, from Withings: http://vitrine-media-cdn.withings.com/wysiwyg/news_events/Withings_Aura_Sleepstudy_250814_US.pdf

Notes

Notes

Notes

Notes

Notes